Town&Co

THE ART OF GRATITUDE
THANK YOU NOTES FOR EVERY OCCASION

Town&Country

The Art of Gratitude

Thank You Notes for Every Occasion

Caroline Tiger

ILLUSTRATIONS BY TANIA LEE

HEARST BOOKS
A division of Sterling Publishing Co., Inc.

New York / London
www.sterlingpublishing.com

Copyright © 2008 by Hearst Communications, Inc.

Designed by Celia Fuller

Library of Congress Cataloging-in-Publication Data

Town & country, the art of gratitude : thank-you notes for every occasion from
the editors of Town & country.
    p. cm.
  Includes bibliographical references and index.
  ISBN-13: 978-1-58816-727-9 (alk. paper)
  ISBN-10: 1-58816-727-5 (alk. paper)
  1. Thank-you notes. I. Town & country. II. Title: Town and country, the art
of gratitude. III. Title: Art of gratitude.
  BJ2115.T45T69 2008
  395.4—dc22

                                        2007045907

10 9 8 7 6 5 4 3 2 1

Published by Hearst Books
A Division of Sterling Publishing Co., Inc.
387 Park Avenue South, New York, NY 10016

Town & Country and Hearst Books are trademarks of Hearst
Communications, Inc.

www.townandcountrymag.com

For information about custom editions, special sales, premium and corporate
purchases, please contact Sterling Special Sales Department at 800-805-5489
or specialsales@sterlingpublishing.com.

Distributed in Canada by Sterling Publishing
c/o Canadian Manda Group, 165 Dufferin Street
Toronto, Ontario, Canada M6K 3H6

Distributed in Australia by Capricorn Link (Australia) Pty. Ltd.
P.O. Box 704, Windsor, NSW 2756 Australia

Printed in USA

Sterling ISBN 13: 978-1-58816-727-9
       ISBN 10: 1-58816-727-5

SPECIAL THANKS

I'd like to thank my mother and father, Jane and Arthur Tiger, for making sure I had personalized notecards from a very young age on which to compose my thank-you notes—and for giving me so much for which to be thankful. I'd also like to thank my English and writing teachers over the years for inspiring a love of reading and writing that fuels my prolificacy with notes and otherwise.

TABLE OF CONTENTS

PAMELA FIORI

Dear Reader,

If you've ever been at a loss for finding exactly the right words to express your appreciation, _The Art of Gratitude_ is for you. From what kind of pen, paper and pencil to use to examples of myriad ways to say "thank you" graciously and gracefully, this little book will help you.

My special thanks goes to its author, Caroline Tiger, who leads the way to a warmer, more courteous means of communication. I suggest you follow her.

Kind Regards,
Pamela Fiori

Town&Country

INTRODUCTION

I receive all kinds of inventive e-cards and e-vites; some as sophisticated as high-budget movies, complete with soundtracks, animated penguins, and rolling credits at the end. My e-mail inbox serves as storage for these and for the dozens of thank-you e-mails that dribble in after I throw a party or sent out a just-because gift. While I salute the creators of these mesmerizing confections and the thoughtfulness behind the thank-you e-mails, I lament that we are chipping away at civilized discourse.

Here's why: When a note is written by hand, more than words are imparted. Consider that each person's handwriting is different; like a hand-hooked rug or a needlepoint sampler, each note bears the mark of its maker. Now, compared to an e-mail where a sender chooses Helvetica or some other font used by millions around the world, you can see, feel, and even smell the difference. By selecting the paper, taking a pen in hand, thinking about what she's going to write, and then connecting pen with paper, a person sends a piece of herself as she was at the moment of the writing. This type of communication forges stronger and more meaningful relationships than those attempted via ephemeral modes such as e-mail or texting.

When you write a thank-you note, you communicate that you have taken time out of a busy day—and our days are only growing busier—to stop and think about why you are grateful. Correspondence transmitted via screens—cell phone, PDA, or computer—is instantaneous and impersonal, with no guarantee that the sender is even who she says she is. The exchange feels more like a transaction—and that's why, when I receive an e-card, I daydream about beautiful stationery and fountain pens forging a firm, unwavering line.

It's only natural that the democratization of technology would lead to what alarmists have termed a thank-you note crisis. One hears horror stories of grade-school children who don't even know how to address an envelope. It's certainly up to the older generations to impart the importance of writing thank-you notes by hand, but there's really no need for an alarm. Once someone has her own supply of stationery—and once she sends a letter and receives one in return—she'll be hooked.

There's no denying the selfish aspects of sending a handwritten note—it's as pleasing for the sender as it is for the recipient. The extravagant paper use might also come into play, but there's no reason to label yourself a tree-killer when there are so many eco-friendly papers in the marketplace. The number of choices continues to grow as consumers become more environmentally aware. Consider limiting your stationery suite to just notecards and letter paper, a perfectly respectable—and even admirable—collection in this technology-centered age.

Let the guidelines set forth in the pages ahead act as your handbook and inspiration. Chapters will discuss your writing tools, the writing basics, and then into your thank-you occasions—weddings, gifts and social occasions, for condolences, from children and teenagers, and business correspondence. Sample letters are provided for you to copy or from which to borrow phrases and ideas.

Thank-you notes aren't only for official occasions, such as wedding gifts or after being hosted at someone's beach house for the weekend. The best thank-you notes come from those impromptu bursts of gratitude—don't keep these to yourself. Pull out a fresh sheet of creamy paper crowned by an elegant monogram, and steal a contemplative moment to think about and appreciate what the recipient of the note means to you.

When you set those thoughts down on paper and drop the note in the post, you will have the chance to revel in the delicious secret that someone out there is going to get her mail in a few days and rifle through the bills and catalogs to find this handmade gift—this instant day-brightener. Who could resist?

CHAPTER 1

Your Tools

YOUR CHOICE OF PAPER, FONT, and language (formal or informal) projects a certain image. Before you select a tool, pause and think about the kind of impression you want to make. Especially because handwritten notes are brief, every detail you offer is a clue to be interpreted. Your thank-you note is expressive on several levels—through its tactile and aesthetic qualities and also through the language you use. Think about what you want to say when you choose your tools: your paper, your printing process, your stationery design, and even your pen.

The Stationery Suite

In this book, we only concern ourselves with the thank-you letter, which is traditionally written on a simple, monogrammed piece that appears as a staple in one's stationery suite or "wardrobe." To a modern-day reader, that old-fashioned phrase might sound odd. Judith Martin aka Ms. Manners quips in her own witty way that when she first heard the words "stationery wardrobe," she thought it meant "dresses that didn't play the trick of looking too short one year and too long the next and that didn't capriciously change their fit throughout the years." Of course, that would be a "stationary wardrobe." A stationery wardrobe refers to the tasteful menagerie of letter paper, note cards, and envelopes that you might find in the writing desk of the most well-appointed lady or gentleman. It's customary to have formal cards, informal fold-over cards, and flat cards—all with matching envelopes; plus white half-sheet paper with engraved monograms; as well as large single sheets with the house address engraved at the top for the use of everyone in the house, including guests.

The details of some traditional stationery components:

Formal letter sheets (5¼ x 7¼): Traditionally white or ecru notepaper made from 100 percent cotton fiber folded vertically, engraved with your monogram, your name only, your address only, or plain. Used for extending and replying to a formal invitation and for writing condolence letters. Use a pen with black ink for a condolence letter.

Informals (5 x 3½): A white or ecru sheet folded horizontally with a person's full name or a couple's name engraved or printed on the front. For writing short notes or as a gift enclosure card.

Message Card (5 x 3½): A single white card with a person's full name or a couple's name engraved in the top center. Used for personal notes, including thank-you notes.

Correspondence cards (6¼ x 4¼): A single card made from weighty stock that can be any color and can be bordered by any color. A monogram, name, or name and address may be engraved at the top center. These are used for writing short notes and for extending and replying to informal invitations.

Half-sheets ($5\frac{3}{4}$ x $7\frac{3}{4}$): The first sheet is engraved or printed with a monogram or name and address and the second sheets are blank. Used for writing letters, these can be white, ecru, pale blue, or pale gray.

Folded Notes ($5\frac{1}{4}$ x $3\frac{1}{2}$): The front page is blank or a monogram is engraved in the center. The paper color is traditionally pale blue, gray, or some other soft color. Used for thank-you notes and other general correspondence.

Today, a lesser suite is appropriate, reducing the amount of paper you will need to have on hand. Most seem to get by with a letter sheet, correspondence cards, fold-over notes, and the accompanying envelopes. What's most important is that both your formal and informal needs are covered. Here's the simplified suite we suggest:

- Letter sheets with your monogram in black ink for writing a condolence letter or replying to a formal invitation.
- Informal letter sheets with your monogram, name, or name and address, and second sheets that are blank, for informal correspondence.
- Correspondence cards in heavy stock in a color of your choice, or with a border, for writing thank-you notes associated with formal and semi-formal occasions, such as weddings, anniversaries, and graduations. These can be personalized with a monogram or with your full name at the top and center.
- Foldover cards in a lighter cardstock to use for short, more informal notes.

When there's a monogram or imprint on the front of the card, the writing may begin on this page. Usually, though, the monogram or imprint is centered on the front of the card, in which case the text should begin at the top of page three (i.e., the bottom half of the interior when the note is lying flat). The note may continue on page four. Page two is not used. If you need more space, use a different type of stationery and enclose it inside; for example, a letter sheet.

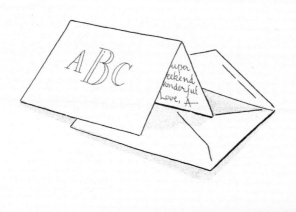

Envelopes

The envelope will make the first impression on the recipient as the frame for your artwork. Envelopes can be purchased individually to complement or to color-coordinate with a particular paper color or style. There are as many envelope types as there are paper choices—they range from highly stylized, such as lined with patterned paper in contrasting colors, to purely practical in all-white or ecru.

Colored linings will go in and out of fashion. We suggest a no-fail style that's always in good taste: a gray tissue lining that matches the monogram or address stamped on the envelope's flap and on the card or letter paper. Colored linings are most suitable for young girls and for particularly festive occasions, but they can also be charming when they match the personality of their owner. They should match the border or color of the type on the stationery, which, as noted above, should never be black.

T&C Tip *It's best to avoid black borders for any piece of stationery because black-edged cards were the traditional format for mourning cards, symbols of remembrance that gained popularity during the Victorian era. During the late 1800s, the demand for mourning ephemera was sufficient enough to merit the need for mourning stockists. Their entire business consisted of supplying funeral cards, funeral programs, artwork, and mourning cards in styles that ranged from simple to elaborate. These cards traditionally featured a photo of the departed along with a biblical verse, a prayer or poem, and often some symbolic artwork such as angels, flowers, or birds.*

Types of Paper and Printing

Who doesn't remember her first visit to a proper stationery store? Inhaling the sweet smell of the paper, flipping through the big binders of samples—letter-sized, flat notes, folded notes, formal and informal—

with every possible combination of font, every shade and texture of paper. And then there are the envelopes, lined with more beautiful paper—marbleized, striped, paisley, and plain.

But how do you choose? The sheer number of paper choices makes selecting the perfect color and cardstock for the right occasion overwhelming. There are as many options for stationery "wardrobes" as there are for fashion wardrobes. Which one is right for you will depend on your lifestyle and how much money you wish to spend.

Papermakers have invented myriad ways to create paper from raw materials than ever before. Soy and bamboo are paper sources now as are many recycled materials. Then there are the classics—cotton fiber and linen. The different material and papermaking processes manifest themselves in the final product's aesthetics, its texture and heft. A paper's form is often defined by its function. You might print the rough draft of a speech on inexpensive, flimsy copy paper. The draft is disposable, so you choose disposable paper. An art monograph is printed on heavy, glossy paper. This book will last forever. It demands a paper with gravitas.

Look to yourself—or in a mirror, at yourself—and at your lifestyle when the time comes to choose your personal stationery. Are you a piece of copy paper or are you an art monograph? The answer will likely lie somewhere in between. Do you intend for your letters to stick around a while? If so, choose a paper made from 100 percent cotton fiber or rag paper, made from cotton cloth. Both are extremely durable.

As always, Emily Post offers some practical advice: "Suitability should be considered in choosing notepaper, as well in choosing a piece of furniture for a house. For a handwriting which is habitually large, a larger sized paper should be chosen than for writing which is small. The shape of the paper should also depend somewhat upon the spacing of the lines which is typical of the writer, and whether a wide or narrow margin is used. Low, spread-out writing looks better on a square sheet of paper; tall, pointed writing looks better on paper that is high and narrow. Selection of paper whether rough or smooth is entirely a matter of personal choice—so that the quality be good, and the shape and color conservative."

Choosing a Stationer

Don't be daunted by the many different types of paper, printing, envelopes, and linings on the market—a good stationer will guide you toward the perfect one for you. Of course, different types of stationers will offer different types of shopping experiences. Your first task must be to select the one that best suits your needs.

LARGE STATIONERY STORE

These stores have the feel of an emporium, and they'll likely carry enormous binders full of samples as well as catalogs from many different manufacturers. They will likely offer competitive pricing, and if you're looking for a traditional, classic, or simple design, this may be the way to go.

The cons? If you're looking for something "outside the box" and creative, a large store might be less able to adapt. (It's harder for an elephant to change direction than it is for a rabbit.) Also, because they carry a wide range of stationery at many different price points, you'll need to educate your eye before you enter be sure that what you're ordering looks and feels like the high-quality stationery that you seek.

INDEPENDENT STATIONERY STORE

It's difficult to survive as a mom-and-pop in a big-box world. Those small stationers that survive must have demonstrated the highest levels of personal service and exquisite taste. Perhaps the stationer who served your mummy and grand-mummy is still around. It's worth checking.

In an independent shop, you're more likely to encounter higher quality and higher pricing. They shouldn't blink at requests for heavily stylistic choices, if that's what you desire. A small stationer will have relationships with other small shops who do engraving and letterpress, as well as with quality calligraphers and monogram designers. The service will be impeccable (hopefully), and you will pay for that with a higher cost.

ONLINE STATIONERS AND MAIL-ORDER CATALOGS

These options are certainly tempting—after all, how convenient is it to sit at home, cozy in your robe, while you choose fonts and select your paper? Unfortunately, the merchandise will often fail to live up to your expectations when it arrives. Since personal stationery is by definition personalized, it will be difficult to return—or re-gift. Additionally, personalizing stationery takes some time, so if you order a suite and are unsatisfied with the results, you will have already lost a few months to the process, and you'll be back at square one. It's best to go to a brick-and-mortar store where you have the option of feeling the paper's heft and running your fingers over the printing samples.

Types of Paper

Once you choose your stationer, the next step is selecting paper.

Cotton fiber: Made from 100-percent cotton. Arguably the most traditional and elegant option.

Handmade papers: Made from natural organic materials including cotton, rag, hemp, and plant fibers; uneven or "rough" in texture.

Laid: Similar to vellum (see page 28), but with a rougher, bumpy finish.

Linen finish: A paper type with a surface that's grainier than pure cotton stocks. Another elegant, classic choice.

Parchment: Cloudy, translucent paper that creates
an airy, poetic effect.

Vellum: Paper made from a cotton blend, with
a translucent, frosted appearance, and a
smooth finish.

Rice paper: A thin, soft paper that's actually not
made from rice. Non traditional, but beautiful
and elegant. It can only accept letterpress
printing.

Rag paper: Made from cotton rags. Extremely durable.

Types of Printing

Your choice of paper will guide your next decision:
the printing type you prefer for the monogram, for
your name, or for some other imprint that will adorn
and personalize your stationery.

Engraving: This method, first introduced in the
seventeenth century, is unparalleled in quality
and elegance. Also called "die-stamping," it's the
epitome of good taste. No other process can
reproduce the particular three-dimensional
quality attained through engraving. More akin
to stamping than to printing, this process begins

with the text etched onto a copper plate or die. The plate is then coated with ink and attached to a press. The press forces the plate into the paper, with much pressure, and the ink is transferred. The effect is slightly raised type—the letter definition is crisp, the ink color is true, and the paper's back is indented or "bruised." Once you've invested in the custom plate, subsequent sets will cost less.

Thermography: Also called "raised printing," thermography results in raised type like engraving but it's less refined—and less expensive. No die is cast and there is no bruise or impression on the paper's back. Instead, the image or letters are printed flat, coated with a powder compound, and passed under a heater. The heat fuses the ink with the compound and the letters or printing will swell to create a three-dimensional effect. Done badly, it can look like stick-on letters. There are two telltale ways to detect thermography from engraving—the ink used in the former is shinier, and unlike engraving, there is no indentation on the back of the paper. Some residue from the process might be left on the pages or inside the envelopes. You may need to blow gently to get rid of the excess powder. Another option available, called "matte thermography," uses a different powder compound and results in a less shiny look.

Letterpress: This labor-intensive technique dates back to the Gutenberg Bible, and the press itself takes up the span of a large walk-in closet. Images or letters are carved into wood blocks and then inked. The paper is pressed into the wood, with less pressure than that applied during engraving, and the images or text are transferred. Letterpress looks especially sharp with modern typefaces.

Offset lithography: This flat process transfers ink from a roller to the paper—an economical way to create a multicolor motif and the most common method of printing.

Embossing: Usually used for large initials or borders, this printing technique forms letters and images with a raised "relief" surface, imparting added dimension.

Blind-embossing: This printing process employs a die (as in engraving) to stamp ink-less letters and images into the surface, causing a raised "relief" effect.

"GRATITUDE UNLOCKS THE FULLNESS OF LIFE. IT TURNS WHAT WE HAVE INTO ENOUGH, AND MORE. IT TURNS DENIAL INTO ACCEPTANCE, CHAOS TO ORDER, CONFUSION TO CLARITY. IT CAN TURN A MEAL INTO A FEAST, A HOUSE INTO A HOME, A STRANGER INTO A FRIEND. GRATITUDE MAKES SENSE OF OUR PAST, BRINGS PEACE FOR TODAY, AND CREATES A VISION FOR TOMORROW." –*Melody Beattie*

Paper and Printing Terms

Here are some more terms you may encounter while you choose your stationery. Refer to this mini-glossary to help you with the unfamiliar lingo.

Calligraphy: Artistic, stylized, or elegant handwriting. Often associated with the elegant, curlicue script found on the most formal of wedding invitations, there are many genres and styles of calligraphy.

Deckle edge: The irregular, feathered, "torn" edge of paper, an effect that can be attained by either machine or by hand. When it's by hand, there are often four deckle edges; when it's by machine, there are two. Typically used on art papers and handmade papers.

Jacquard: Screen-printed paper that creates an illusion of layering; for example, paper that looks like it's overlaid with a swatch of lace.

Typeface: The style/appearance of a letter or numeral. With the arrival of desktop publishing, the term is more or less synonymous with the word "font."

Stock: The term used to describe thickness and heaviness of paper. Heavy card stock is ideal for formal correspondence cards. Lighter stock works better for letter sheets.

Watermark: The translucent emblem or "beauty mark" pressed into fine paper that becomes visible when the paper is held up to a light. A watermark denotes superb quality, signifying the exclusivity of the paper manufacturer or stationer.

Monograms

Monogrammed stationery telegraphs sophistication and elegance. It's also extremely convenient because, like a pair of creamy pearl stud earrings, it complements everything, whether formal or informal. If you do decide to monogram, you have the option of one, two, or three initials.

The most common monogram has three—a pair of initials (the first initial of the first and middle names) the same size flanking the larger initial (the first initial of the surname) in the center. A single or married woman who keeps her maiden name uses the initials of her first, middle, and last names. A married woman who takes her husband's name uses the initials of her first, maiden, and husband's last names. A standard stationer can create this monogram and may offer other options as well.

You can also commission a designer or design your own. There are all sorts of inventive modern versions of the classic monogram; in cursive topped with a crown, embedded in a leaf or rosette, in block Art Deco–style letters. Even the classic design has options; it can be shaped like a diamond or oval, fixed within a border, or floating in white space. Select the one that suits you.

If you choose to print your name on stationery instead of selecting a monogram, here's how it should appear:

Single woman:
Holly Jones
Miss Holly Jones

—————

Married woman who keeps her maiden name:
Mrs. Holly Jones
Holly Jones

Married woman who takes her husband's name:
Mrs. Justin Mickelson
Mrs. Holly Mickelson
Holly Mickelson

A married woman who is a doctor:
Doctor Holly Mickelson
Dr. Holly Mickelson

Divorced woman who has taken
her husband's name:
Mrs. Holly Mickelson
Ms. Holly Mickelson
Holly Mickelson

Further Flourishes

There are many ways to decorate stationery beyond the traditional letterhead and monogram. If you step foot in one of the large stationery stores, you'll be overwhelmed—and possibly seduced—by the monogram embossing stamps, stickers, wax seals,

T&C Tip: *A man's stationery is more conservative than a woman's, with his name engraved without a title unless he is an M.D., in which case he uses "Dr." or a member of the clergy or military. Gothic and Roman are the traditional fonts used for a man's letter sheets or correspondence cards.*

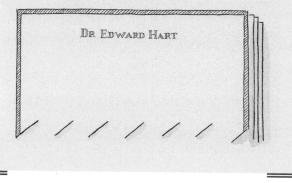

DR. EDWARD HART

and stencils. If you decide to add any of these flourishes to your letter sheet, card, or envelope, be careful not to draw attention away from your written message. Only use them to creatively add one or two decorative touches—"touch" being the operative word. A simpler aesthetic that doesn't overpower the hallmarks of quality—a thick paper, a gorgeous engraving job—will always communicate a more powerful and elegant message.

Pre-printed Cards

Boxed sets of cards are available from quality stationers that say "Thank You" on the front. There are also entire sections in drugstore greeting-card aisles dedicated to the thank-you card. The latter is acceptable for children or possibly for when you want to send a humorous note. The former—the boxed notes—are actually less useful than boxes of plain notepaper or cards of premium stock. The front-and-center placement of the words "Thank You" detracts from your own written message, and the ownership of such cards indicates that you only pen notes when you have someone to thank.

In fact, it has traditionally been a hallmark of a person who is in good social standing to write notes on all occasions; to look after a friend's well-being, to RSVP, to invite, to send a clipping from a newspaper, to communicate condolences or an apology. This extensive list of reasons to write demonstrates the futility of a box of stationery with a single purpose.

Pen and Ink

You may not think that the recipient of your letter or card will know which type of pen you used, but that's not so. Marks made by a ballpoint pen appear much different than those made by a fountain pen. One floats on the surface of the paper and the other deposits ink deep into its tiny crevices. More importantly, your choice of pen dictates your own writing ease. A well-made fountain pen or a calligraphy pen might entice you to your writing desk while a standard ballpoint incites no such eagerness for the task at hand.

Fountain pens grew in popularity in the nineteenth century, and in 1938, a Hungarian journalist invented the ballpoint pen. Today, luckily for us, we have many options. Most of us are multi-pen people, with ballpoints for note-taking and fountain pens for letter-writing. Results will differ depending on the type of pen, paper material, and paper thickness. You will need to experiment to match pen with the paper—and pen with personality.

Of course, once the pen is chosen, the ink may still be in question. Pens come in a slew of colors. It's fun to experiment with different ones, but for note-writing, blue or black is best. Green and red should be reserved for holiday cards. Silver and sparkles should be reserved for children.

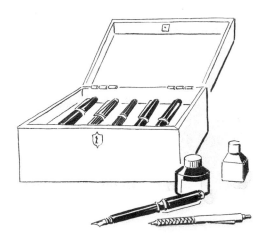

YOUR TOOLS

> T&C Factoid: *For more than 1,000 years, the writing instrument of choice was the quill pen, made from bird feathers. For luxury, people chose quills made from swan feathers, but crows' feathers actually provided the finest line.*

Organizing your Paper

It's said that Princess Diana kept her paper on her desk to remind her to write thank-you notes before she retired to the bedroom. Storing a few sheets and envelopes out in the open and the rest in one or more containers near your desk is a good strategy.

Choosing the container can be just as much fun as choosing the stationery. Find a box that you like that matches your décor. You may have to buy a bigger box once your stationery collection grows to include different types of formal and informal notes. Make sure that your paper lies flat inside the stationery box. You never want to store paper on its edge or with any edges hanging over—it runs the risk

Postmarks and Stamps

Is there a post office nearby that offers a special historic postmark? The floor of the B. Free Franklin Post Office in Philadelphia's Old City is often stacked with boxes of wedding invitations waiting to receive the special handwritten Franklin postmark. Brides send their invites and thank-you notes to Loveville, Maryland; Romance, Arizona; or Loveland, Colorado to be postmarked. If you're a bride, and you'd like to try this yourself: Send your notes with adequate self-addressed stamped envelopes, and specify that you are "re-mailing" the envelopes. The post office will apply the postmark and send them back. Another bridal option is to seek out the calligraphic dove-and-heart stamps issued by the United States Postal Service for wedding correspondence.

The service called Photostamps allows you to upload a digital photo and buy authorized stamps from the postal service. This is another wonderful and creative way to personalize thank-you notes for gifts. A bride and groom might use a photo from their honeymoon. Thanks-you notes for a child's birthday gifts might feature a photostamp of the child eating birthday cake or wearing a birthday hat. Keep in mind that such creative flourishes are not appropriate for somber occasions, such as sending thanks for condolences.

of rippling or curling. Another important concern is to keep your paper cool and dry, as moisture can cause curling or make the adhesive on the envelopes moisten and stick. Be especially careful of storage if you live in a humid climate. The ideal temperature is 75 degrees or less—and stationery should always be kept out of direct sunlight.

If you have room, designate one area to be a writing area, and install a writing desk with a comfortable chair and pleasing lamp. Leave everything there so you know where to find it, and so everything—including paper, pen, stamps, and addresses—is in one place when you need it. A blotter on the desktop will provide a smooth writing foundation and protect the surface of the desk.

For those with less-than-legible handwriting

It's possible, no matter your age, to improve your handwriting. It simply takes time and patience. Often when people have difficulty it stems from the way they hold their pen and the muscles they use to write. Those with better handwriting use their shoulder and forearm muscles to write and hold their fingers and wrist stiff. Those who don't write legibly typically use their fingers and wrist to move the pen; they need to learn to isolate these muscles and use their larger muscles instead. Take out some sheets of paper and practice writing, first to see which muscles you're using, and second, to try to correct your stance. Try this sentence: "The quick brown fox jumps over the lazy dog." See the Appendix on page 151 for more assistance.

Conclusion

With all of the details involved in selecting paper, a type of printing, and your pen, it's easy to lose sight of the forest for the trees. Remember, what's most important is the sentiment of gratitude; you are truly thankful for the gesture or gift imparted by the recipient of your note. You are sending them an acknowledgment of their kindness in a conscientious and expressive manner.

"NEVER THINK, BECAUSE YOU CANNOT WRITE A LETTER EASILY, THAT IT IS BETTER NOT TO WRITE AT ALL. THE MOST AWKWARD NOTE IMAGINABLE IS BETTER THAN NONE—FOR TO WRITE NONE IS THE DEPTH OF RUDENESS, WHEREAS THE AWKWARD NOTE MERELY FAILS TO DELIGHT." *–Emily Post*

CHAPTER TWO

The Basics of Writing Thank-yous

N O ONE IS BORN A SKILLED writer of thank-you notes. As with most proficiencies, this comes with practice and time, and there is always time to thank people for their gifts and kindnesses. Happily there are some basic guidelines to ensure that we don't begin the process in the dark.

First, some thank-you note dos and don'ts:

Do:

- Match the thank-you to the gesture. Thank a friend for a fun cocktail party with an upbeat note written on your casual stationery. Thank a respected colleague for a referral with a substantive letter written on your monogrammed letter paper.
- It's never too early but it's often too late. Write the thank you note as soon as possible.
- Make certain you're thanking the correct person. If the name on the gift card is illegible, ask the people in question before you write the note.
- Be specific in your gratitude. A general thank-you does not seem sincere; mention the gesture specifically and also how you feel about it and when you plan to use it.
- Do include the date.

Don't:

- If you are late, don't apologize for it in the first line. Keep the emphasis on gratitude.

- Never second-guess a thank-you note. It's always appropriate.
- Never misspell the recipient's name.
- Don't over-thank. Exuding enthusiasm often feels false and insincere to the recipient.
- Don't cross out and correct errors in your note. Rewrite it.
- Don't use stationery that has "thank you" already printed on it. The more sophisticated choice is blank stationery or stationery printed with a name or monogram.

On Which Occasions

Some instances that call for thank-you notes are obvious—for a wedding, birth, graduation, or birthday gift; for hosting a houseguest or throwing a dinner party; for condolences after a death in the family. In the business world, thank-notes should be written after referrals, job interviews, and references. Those who donate to fund-raising events should receive thank-you notes. Then there are thank-yous that are charming because they are unexpected; these are the thank-yous that we write for no

special occasion to the people who have made a difference in our lives—to a good friend, a cherished parent, a reliable employee, or a supportive wife.

Sitting Down to Write

I once heard a professional writer confess her fear of the blank page and the menacing blinking cursor. I think everyone—even those who are paid to write—are intimidated by that first step. No one is born a proficient letter writer. It comes with time and plenty of practice—which is, by the way, a great argument for starting children early.

Pretending you're not writing the letter for *real* is often an effective trick. Pull out a piece of notepaper—as opposed to your lovely, monogrammed fold-over notes—and start jotting down ideas. Since this is just practice, you can relax and write what comes to mind. Your words should say what you mean, which requires getting specific. Anyone can write a generic note that says, "Thank you for the lovely gift." The trick is thinking of something original and finishing with grace.

Words and phrases to get you started:
Your kindness means so much.
I'll never forget your thoughtfulness.
Thank you for your thoughtful hospitality.
Your kindness is like a ray of sunlight on a dreary day.
Thank you for making us feel like we're part of
    the family.
It was so thoughtful of you to think of us.
It's hard to decide which was better—your company
    or your delicious food.
Your thoughtfulness meant more than words can
    ever say.

Whenever I look at the gift you gave me, I'll think
fondly of you.

Thank you for your support and understanding.

With sincere gratitude for all you've done.

Your gift has already become a treasured keepsake.

Your gift will always remind us of this special time
in our lives.

Thank you for helping me follow my dreams.

I am so lucky to have you as a friend.

Thank you for your generous gift. We plan to use it
toward the down-payment on our house.

We had a lovely time visiting your home last weekend.

What a delightful party!

It's just what I've always needed.

Your gift brightens up the living room.

It's just the right color for the den.

Writing Tips

While beginning with "Thank you for the [blank]"
can occasionally be fine, there are options. Try drawing the reader into the letter with a sentence beginning with "I" or "You" or with a person's or people's
reactions: "I was overjoyed to receive your lovely

gift," "You've outdone yourself this year," "We had so much fun last night," "I've always wanted this magazine," "The kids were so excited when they saw you'd sent a gift." You can even start by naming whatever it is you're thanking them for: "The sweater is perfect," "Your party was the most fun we've had in ages," "How did you know that Naples was the one city in Italy that was missing from my snow globe collection?"

If you're stuck, think of the giver. Imagine her picking out the gift. What was her thought process as she chose this gift for you? What does she mean to you? What would you say to her if you were face-to-face? Grab a photo of that person if you have one, or just imagine her sitting across from you. This will help you maintain a friendly and conversational tone, as all good notes should read. Try to tie the gift to the person. If she gave you a cheeseboard, does she have a lovely cheeseboard that you've admired? Is she a cheese aficionado? Think of the gift. This is another key to cracking the code of the thank-you note. Was it something you've always wanted? Was it something you didn't know you wanted or needed until you received it? If it's an article of clothing or a piece of jewelry, does it bring out the color of your eyes or complement the rest of your collection? (Note: If it's something you neither want nor need, avoid brainstorming in this direction. Try to find the good in the gift or at least in the giving of the gift.)

When the Gift Isn't to Your Liking

This might be the most difficult thank-you note to write. When you can't find anything redeeming about the gift, it behooves you to tap into your creative well and strive to convincingly make fiction sound like nonfiction. Remind yourself that the gift itself isn't of the greatest import—the phrase "it's the thought that counts," is no less true for being well-worn. While you craft your note, focus on the thoughtfulness of the giver rather than on the hideous ceramic knick-knack or the rhinestone-studded t-shirt. The basic format shouldn't stray far from the customary format. Finding the good in the gift means finding the good in the person who sent it, and focusing on that.

Here are some sentiments to get you started:

You have such delightful/eclectic/unique taste in picture frames.

You always send the most unforgettable gifts.

The last thing Jon and I were expecting in today's mail was a [ ].

You were so thoughtful to think of me.

I can only imagine how much trouble you went to find this [very unusual picture frame]. I'm so appreciative of your time and your well-wishes.

"I WOULD MAINTAIN THAT THANKS ARE THE HIGHEST FORM OF THOUGHT, AND THAT GRATITUDE IS HAPPINESS DOUBLED BY WONDER." –*G.K. Chesterton*

Dear Priscilla,

I'm writing to thank you for the vintage dress-form that you sent to me and Jeff as a housewarming present. It was so clever of you to think of the history of our building as a former dress-making factory when you were picking out our gift. You're incredibly resourceful—I can't imagine where you found it! We so appreciate your creativity and your thoughtful consideration, and we look forward to welcoming you to our new apartment when you're in town next month. We missed you at the housewarming party.

Fondly,
Kimberly

Appropriate Forms of Address

"Dear" and the name of whomever you're writing is the customary way to begin a thank-you note. Whether or not you use someone's first name or her surname with a title or honorific depends on your relationship. If you're a teenager thanking a parent's friend for a graduation gift, you need to use a more formal salutation. If you're a teenager thanking a friend for the cool skateboard he gave you on your birthday, the first name will do.

When in doubt, for example in business situations, take your cue from the other person. See how they sign their own letters, and mimic the way they've signed their name while addressing your own correspondence.

Exceptions to "Dear" are "Darling" and "Dearest" for loved ones. If you're writing a general letter and you don't know who will be opening it, "To Whom It May Concern" is more practical than "Dear Sirs" or "Dear Madam," since you have no way of knowing the recipient's gender.

The Basic Format

There are ways to embellish each of these basic building blocks, but in many cases just the following will do nicely:

Salutation

Dear Aunt Vera,

———

Mention the gift or kindness right away.

What a treat to receive your lovely flowers this morning. OR Your lovely flowers were delivered this morning.

———

Personalize the note by saying how you feel about it. Why does the gift suit you? Why are you deriving such pleasure from it? Be specific.

I don't have to tell you that white roses are my favorite bloom. I'm sure you can picture how beautifully they dress up my office. I put them there so I can look at them all day.

———————

Say "thank you."

Thanks a million for the beautiful bouquet.

———————

The wind-up sentence.

I very much look forward to seeing you at Dad's next week.

———————

Closing

Much love,
Sarah

The entire note looks like this:

Dear Aunt Vera,

What a treat to receive your lovely flowers this morning. I don't have to tell you that white roses are my favorite bloom. I'm sure you can picture how beautifully they dress up my office. I put them there so I can look at them all day.

Thanks a million for the beautiful bouquet. I very much look forward to seeing you at Dad's next week.

Much love,
Sarah

Closings

Whereas "Dear" is the one-and-only opener, the list of options for closing a letter are long and nuanced. Select your closing based on the letter's formality and on your relationship with the recipient. Err on the side of formality, and steer away from closings that could just as easily close an e-mail or text message, such as "Hugs," "SWAK," and "XOXO."

Close friends/family members:

Love

Much love

Fondly

Affectionately

As ever

Lesser friends and relatives:

Warmly	As ever
All best	With love
All the best	Yours
Best	

Acquaintances and business-related thank-you notes:
Sincerely
Respectfully
Sincerely yours
Respectfully yours
Best wishes
Kindest regards
Gratefully

A Note on Postscripts

If one more thought pops into your head after you've already "signed off," and if it's something you feel you must include, it's possible to add a postscript. A better option is ripping up the note and starting again, this time weaving the new information into the main message. Sometimes, though, we're in a terrible hurry or we're down to our last piece of paper. In these cases, a postscript has to do. It should be preceded by the letters "P.S." and should be kept to one sentence. If you need to write more, or if you need a second postscript—a "P.P.S."—it's best to write a second note in a few days or make a follow-up phone call.

How To Vary the Tone To Suit the Occasion

The salutation and closing contribute to communicating a certain tone. Other ways to alter the tone of the letter include your choice of language, use of contractions, the types of references or allusions made in the letter, and the type of stationery on which the letter is written. Think of the person to whom you're writing. Is she playful? Does she have a strong sense of humor? Or is she more straight-laced and conservative in their actions and language? While the note should reflect your own personality, it should also be enjoyable for the recipient. Be sensitive to them.

"AS WE EXPRESS OUR GRATITUDE,
WE MUST NEVER FORGET THAT THE HIGHEST
APPRECIATION IS NOT TO UTTER WORDS, BUT
TO LIVE BY THEM." –*John F. Kennedy*

Dear Mom,

It was so cool to get your package at the dorm today. It made my day. When I opened it up to find a box of your awesome oatmeal cookies plus a special coffee mug and a bag of my favorite coffee, I felt like I was home again. I miss you, and the dogs. Thanks, Mom, and I'll see you in a few weeks.

> *Love,*
> *Jack*

Dear Emma,

I was so happy to come home from work and find something in the mail other than bills and junk mail. It was an envelope from you, decorated with one of your signature flowers—a treat in itself. When I opened it and found the gift certificate to my favorite bookstore, I was absolutely tickled. The new Sue Grafton mystery is out, and I have been wanting to read it. I am going to the store tonight to pick it up.

Thank you so much!

All my love,
Allison

E-mail

E-mail has largely replaced the phone call and most especially the thank-you note and other handwritten correspondence, and this is not okay. Any act traditionally answered with a thank-you note—be it a gift, a kind gesture, or a condolence letter—requires thoughtfulness and consideration. Replying to their act with an e-mail, by definition extemporaneous and impersonal no matter how many emoticons and XOs, is not an equal effort. If time is of the essence, an e-mail or a phone call are adequate stopgap measures (especially in business correspondence; see page 139), but both should always be followed by a handwritten note.

Addressing Envelopes

If the letter is handwritten, the envelope should be handwritten. If the letter is typed—not recommended for social correspondence—the envelope can still be handwritten. Handwriting an envelope makes the receipt of the letter more exciting—think of what a delight it is when you spy a handwritten envelope tucked in the stack of generic junk mail, catalogs, and bills.

The recipient's name and address should be centered and either flush left or with each line indented slightly more than the one preceding it. The city, state, and zip code are all on the same line. Of course, the writing should be legible. We've all received letters from those so skilled at penmanship that their lines of text look as if they were written with the help of a ruler. This is admirable, but not required; just take care to make sure the lines don't swoop up- or downward too dramatically. Your return address

should be engraved or printed on the back flap, so it can easily be torn off and saved. Traditionally, numbers that appear in the address are spelled out, i.e., 422 East Twenty-third Street. But today this is only true for the most formal correspondence, and the informal style, 422 East 23rd Street, is accepted.

Other traditional rules have similarly relaxed, including writing out all numbers from one to ten, spelling out middle names, and spelling out the full names of states. Today numerals, initials for middle names—if that's what the recipient uses herself—and the official two-letter abbreviations for state names are all appropriate. Do use abbreviations for titles, such as Mr. and Mrs. Here are some suggestions for specific situations:

Girls twelve or younger:
Miss Anna Hirsch
Anna Hirsch
(letter begins with "Dear Anna")

Girls thirteen to twenty:
Miss Anna Hirsch
(letter begins with "Dear Anna")

———————

Ladies twenty-one and older:
Ms. Anna Hirsch

———————

Boys seventeen or younger:
Louis Osbourne
(letter begins with "Dear Louis")

———————

Men eighteen and older:
Mr. Louis Osbourne

———————

To Jr., Sr., III, and 4th:
Mr. Kip Millstone, Jr. (if spelled out,
"j" and "s" are lowercase)
Mr. Kip Millstone III
Mr. Kip Millstone 4th

To an Esquire (i.e., attorney):
Barbara Napp, Esq.
Barbara Napp, Esquire
(letter begins with "Dear Mrs. Napp" or
"Dear Ms. Napp")

To an Esquire and a spouse who's not a lawyer:
Mr. and Mrs. Michael Napp

To a doctor:
Doctor Phil Platt
Dr. Phil Platt

Doctor married to a nondoctor spouse:
Dr. Polly Platt and Mr. Phil Platt

To two married doctors:
The Doctors Platt
Doctor (Dr.) Polly Platt
and Doctor (Dr.) Phil Platt
Doctors (Drs.) Polly and Phil Platt

To two married doctors when the wife
goes by her maiden name:
Dr. Polly Apfelbaum and Dr. Phil Platt

Widow:
A widow does not change her name
from when she was married.

While the envelope calls for formal address and the use of various titles, the inside letter doesn't need to stand by such ceremony. Address the actual note or letter as befits your relationship with the recipient. A friend or relative is called by his first name ("Dear Phillip"); a professor, a friend of a parent, or other category of elder is addressed as Professor, Dr., Mr., and so forth.

Envelope Flaps

Most envelopes made during the nineteenth century featured a teardrop-shaped flap, but today these are not in wide use. In fact, there aren't very many options within the category of envelope-flap styles.

Here are the choices:

Pointed flap: The most elegant, traditional and formal style—also called a "Baronial" envelope.

Square flap: Provides a younger, more contemporary appearance—and a larger area for designs or for return addresses that are printed in a larger typeface.

Deckle edge: Used only when the paper is also made with a deckle, or torn, edge and only with square flaps.

CHAPTER THREE

Weddings and Related Events

I F YOU'RE NOT ALREADY PRACTICED at writing thank-you notes, a wedding will turn you into an instant expert. There are so many occasions at which you'll be gifted, wished well, toasted, and celebrated. All of these deserve thanks.

The Stationery

Your thank-you notes should look as if they come from the same stationer as your wedding invitations. Use the same paper and strike the same overall tone with the design. If the invitations were classic and tailored, the thank-you notes should be as well.

Designing Your Monogram as a Couple

An invitation designer can design a custom monogram for a bride and groom to adorn anything and everything having to do with the wedding. (You can even monogram your cake.) Some use the monogram as a consistent design element that ties together all the correspondence, from the save-the-date cards to the thank-you notes. A couple's monogram usually includes the first letter of the bride's first name and the first letter of the groom's first name flanking the last letter of the groom's last name. If the bride chooses to keep her name, a lovely two-letter monogram might make more sense and is a possibility. If the bride plans to change her name and wants to use her own monogram with her new married name on correspondence, she should only do so after

> E C M
>
> Dear Lisa,
> We were delighted that you
> could be there with us during
> this very special moment in our
> lives. It meant so much to see

the ceremony has occurred and she is officially Mrs. Whomever.

Thank-you Notes and Wedding Etiquette

Wedding thank-you guidelines are similar to those for everyday thank-you notes, just larger in scope. The list of thank-yous to write during and after a wedding season far surpasses the short list of thank-yous to write following, for example, a minor birthday. For this reason, your wedding thank-yous might be uniformly brief, but they should still be personal and thoughtful. Even during a wedding weekend packed with events, the bride and groom might not have a chance to speak with every guest. The thank-you note gives them this chance.

Every person who sends the bride and groom a gift should receive a thank-you note, regardless of whether they attended the ceremony or reception, as well as those who sent a congratulation card or a note wishing the new couple well. The gifts mentioned include gifts for all wedding-related events, from the engagement and rehearsal dinner to the bachelor party and bridal luncheon. In addition, the bride and groom should write thank-you notes— and, if they wish, give thank-you gifts—to their attendants. A thank-you note to the parents and the in-laws is appropriate, especially if they've contributed toward the financing of the event.

The basics:
Write them right away. There are several reasons for promptness. Thank-you notes let the gift giver know that his or her gift has arrived. Don't keep the gift giver on pins and needles wondering if you've received the gift or if the card fell off. Also, it's best to keep on top of things and to

send the notes out while the occasion is still fresh in your mind. This allows you to more easily capture the moment in your prose. While this can be difficult, if you have a few days between the wedding and your departure for the honeymoon, send a few before you go. No newlywed wants to return from her honeymoon to such a gargantuan task.

The exception. If you received the gift before the wedding, wait until after the wedding to send the thank-you note. Sending notes this early is certainly admirable for its conscientiousness but can be a bit jarring for the gift giver.

If you can't write them right away... Send your notes before one month has passed since the gift was given.

Keep track. The best way to record gifts is track them as they arrive. Start with copies of your invitation lists and write your notes next to the guest's name. Record any details that will come in handy when you're writing your thank-you note, such as the color and quantity, first impression, whether their card says anything particularly personal or clever, and whether the card was signed by their guest. In the second column, indicate when a thank-you note goes out to that gift giver. Use a simple word-processing application to create a table on your computer.

An example:

Guests	Gift	Signed by	Notes
Shannon Weatherly & Phil Lingon	red Kitchen Aid mixer	Shannon & Phil (guest)	We admired theirs when we visited Boston last spring and they had us over for dinner — Shannon made those amazing mashed potatoes with the mixer.

Divide and conquer. The bride and groom should share this task—he writes the notes to his family and friends and she takes care of hers. If there are people who are friends of both, the bride and groom should both sign those notes.

Keep it simple. Write five to six lines on stationery that matches or complements your wedding invitations. Remember to personalize each note and mention specifics about the gift and why you like it, and what you plan to use it for in the future. If the gift was money, specify what you plan to use it for, perhaps a down payment on a new house or for the honeymoon.

"APPRECIATION CAN MAKE A DAY, EVEN CHANGE A LIFE. YOUR WILLINGNESS TO PUT IT INTO WORDS IS ALL THAT IS NECESSARY." –*Margaret Cousins*

FOR A SHOWER GIFT:

Dear Alison,

I know you witnessed my excitement first-hand when I opened your gift at the shower, but allow me to tell you again how much I love the beautiful nesting bowls. They already have a place of honor on a shelf in the kitchen where I (and, eventually, Robert) will be able to see them every day.

I'm so happy you made it to the shower. It wouldn't have been the same without you there.

Fondly,
Marge

FOR WEDDING GIFTS FROM DEAR
FRIENDS AND CLOSE FAMILY MEMBERS:

Dear Aunt Joan and Uncle David,

Michael and I were excited when we saw your return address. You have a reputation in our household as being skillful giftgivers. This time you really outdid yourselves. The Kosta Boda vase is absolutely stunning. It may even inspire us to begin a collection as impressive as the many beautiful collections you've acquired over the years. We hope you can visit soon, so we can show you the vase in its place of honor. We put it in the center of our mantel, so we can see it every day.

Much love,
Emma and Michael

WEDDINGS AND RELATED EVENTS

Dear Nancy and Jack,

By traveling all that way to attend the wedding, you've touched our hearts. And with your thoughtful gift, you've touched our palates! In a few days we are off to our honeymoon in Italy, where I know we will find some lovely wine to pour into your beautiful wineglasses. Rest assured, they will be put to good use—and we look forward to having you over to take them for a test run. A thousand thanks.

Love,
Bridget and Henry

Dear Kristine and Jon,

Well, we had no idea what sorts of tricks you two had up your sleeves. Watching you get down to James Brown (pictures to follow) was a highlight of the evening. That virtuoso performance is only topped by your fabulous gift. We are already enjoying sleeping between our sumptuous Frette linens. But most of all, we thank you for being such wonderful friends. It meant a great deal to see your smiling faces— and your dancing feet—at our wedding.

Much love,
Harriet and Pete

Dear Uncle Andrew,

Thank you so much for the lovely candle-sticks. They are exquisite, and we plan to use them not just on special occasions, but every day so we can enjoy them. We hope you can come visit soon so we can share them with you, too.

It was so kind of you to come all the way to San Francisco for the wedding. We were so happy to see you.

With all our love,
Karen and Patrick

"Gratitude is not only the greatest of virtues,

but the parent of all the others."

–Marcus Tuillius Cicero

FOR WEDDING GIFTS FROM
ACQUAINTANCES OR RELATIVES YOU
DON'T KNOW AS WELL:

Dear Jane,

The lovely porcelain Nantucket basket you sent already has a place of honor on our mantel. We walk past it every day—and every day it reminds us of our favorite place in the world. Thank you so much for the thoughtful gift.

Warm regards,
Brooke and Kevin

Dear Mr. Bendel,

We were so happy that you traveled all the way from Turkey to share our joy. It truly meant so much to us to see you there. And on top of it, a lovely engraved silver platter! You are so generous, and we thank you for this beautiful keepsake.

> *Most affectionately,*
> *Caren and Paul*

———

Dear Corrine,

Clink! That's the sound of our brand-new and quite exquisite wineglasses as we toast you and your wonderful gift. Thank you for the glasses and for sharing our special day.

> *All our best,*
> *Gabby and David*

FOR A GIFT OF MONEY:

Dear Nancy,

Thank you so much for your generous gift. John and I are going to use the sum toward a down payment on a house. We're already scouring the real-estate ads. We look forward to having you over once we are in and settled. Thanks again for helping us start our life together and for being at the wedding—it meant a lot to us to see you there.

Affectionately,
Kendra and Bill

FOR A GIFT YOU DON'T CARE FOR:

Dear Dr. and Mrs. Leigh,

Greg and I want to thank you for the neon sign that spells out our names. We still haven't figured out a good place for it. We think that when we move into the new house, it might be the perfect thing to hang above our bar. It's certainly a creative gift, and it's something we never would've splurged on ourselves. Thanks again for thinking of us.

Fondly,
Melissa and Greg

Dear Sally and Seth,

Jon and I want to thank you from the bottoms of our hearts for the amazing engagement party you hosted in our honor last Saturday. We had so much fun. The evening was full of so many wonderful surprises. We can't even imagine the gargantuan effort that went into compiling all of those photos of us from every stage of life. The slideshow was hilarious, and your toast is making me well up again now, just thinking about it. Thank you, thank you, thank you. We hope that one day soon, we can return the favor.

Much love,
Kristine and Kyle

Dear Melissa,

It meant so much to me that you were part of my and Hamish's big day. Actually, as a bridesmaid, you were much more than a part of that one day or weekend—you were a great support and help to me during the many days leading up to it. You've been a cherished friend to me for many years—can you believe how long it's been since we met that fateful day in the fall of upper-mid year? Are we that old?— and I know that we'll remain friends for much longer. We have to, after all. I know all of your secrets!

Thanks for being a picture-perfect bridesmaid, inside and out.

Love always,
Jennifer

Dear Ken,

Thank you for being our ring bearer at the wedding. You did such a good job, and you looked so handsome. It is a day we will remember forever, and it was made even more special because of you.

   Thanks, buddy!

            With all our love,
            Laura and Shawn

"LIZZIE AND I WILL EVER THINK OF YOU AT OUR SOUP; AND I SHALL ALWAYS POUR OUT A LIBATION FROM THE TUREEN TO THE ANGELIC DONOR, BEFORE HELPING A MERE VULGAR BROTH-BIDDING MORTAL LIKE MYSELF."

–Herman Melville thanking his cousin, Catherine Lansing, for a soup ladle, 1872

TO THE PARENTS:

Dear Mom and Dad,

What can we say? Thank you doesn't quite cut it, but it's a start. You helped put together one of the most special days of our entire lives. From supporting our engagement and guiding us through the preparations to looking so great and being there with us through everything, we just can't tell you enough how much we love you and appreciate you.

Love,
Shannon and Mark

CHAPTER FOUR

Gifts and Other Gestures

T HANK-YOU NOTES FOR GIFTS and gestures should reflect the situation at hand. You would write a thank-you note for a priceless heirloom given on a formal occasion on formal stationery to acknowledge the generosity of the gift giver as well as how valuable the gift is and how well it will be cared for. A note thanking someone for a spontaneous bouquet of flowers will look different; this can be penned on more casual stationery and the tone will be short and sweet, just like the beautiful, ephemeral gift it honors.

Gift Giving

Even if the person was present when you opened her gift and she witnessed your excitement and gratitude firsthand, write a thank-you note. There's no scenario in which a person should not receive a note for giving a gift. They've gone to the trouble, and so should you. In the note, think about the enthusiasm you felt upon opening the gift, and articulate why it suits you so well.

When you receive money, don't mention the amount in your thank-you letter. The number is not something that should concern you during the writing of the note since you are really thanking them for the gesture and for their thoughtfulness.

A FORMAL THANK-YOU FOR A GIFT:

Dear Mr. and Mrs. Whitehall,

*Thank you so much for your generous gradua-
tion gift. As you know I'm matriculating to law
school in a few months, and this will be a great
help as I purchase all of the books and supplies
I need to prepare for my three-year stint in New
Haven. Again, many thanks for thinking of me.*

Fondly,
Derek

"WORDS, ONCE THEY ARE PRINTED,
HAVE A LIFE OF THEIR OWN." *–Carol Burnett*

Dear Alistair,

The gift certificate for the French Laundry is really such an amazing gift. The only problem is, once I use it, I'll no longer have something so delectable in my future! Still, I'll find a way. Thanks so much for your generosity, for your foodie know-how, and for thinking of me on my birthday.

Much love,
Justine

Dear Alex,

So many thanks for the beautiful photo album. Peter, the kids, and I are about to take our annual Bermuda trip, so I will certainly have plenty of snapshots to fill its pages. I look forward to showing you the whole kit and kaboodle when we return in August.

I was so glad you were able to make it to the party. It's always such a treat to see you.

Warmest regards,
Susan

Dear Allison,

I can't wait to bundle my baby in the beautiful blanket you gave me. I especially like the lambs that are embroidered on it! Because it has blue, pink, and yellow in it, it will go perfectly with any color scheme I select for the baby's room. (I'm a little behind in that!)

This is such an exciting time for me, and I give thanks every day that I have a friend like you to share it with. Twelve more weeks and I'll be a mom!

Lots of love,
Deborah

Dinner Parties

A note of thanks is in good taste, even if you contributed a bottle of wine or a dessert to the meal. Write not only about the food but also about the company at dinner. Compliment the host or hostess on the whole experience, including the well-engineered social mix.

If a couple visits another couple, the note doesn't have to be from both to both, but everyone should be mentioned in the letter.

Dear Jen,

On the way home, neither Bob nor I could remember the last time we had as much fun as we did at your apartment last night. Jeff has really come a long way as a bartender—he mixes a mean Cosmo. The scalloppini was truly heavenly. And your friends, the Calebs, are delightful. Thanks to you and Jeff for including us in a wonderful evening.

As ever,
Gayle

Dear Lisa,

You truly outdid yourself last night. We just couldn't get enough of that gorgeous food. You're going to have to give me the recipe for your roasted chicken. And the company was wonderful—Jon and I really loved seeing the Joneses again. Barry tells the funniest stories. Thanks to you and Tom for having the wonderful idea to bring us all together, and for making the evening so delectable.

Warmly,
Candace

Dear Hal and April,

We had such a wonderful time last night! Everything was special, from the first drink on the patio to the very last spoonful of tiramisu. The food just got better and better as the night went on. And the company was great fun. It was lovely to get to know Bill and Sue a bit better. The combination of that gorgeous mozzarella and their stories about touring the Amalfi Coast have me dreaming of visiting Italy—and soon. Thanks so much for a fabulous evening.

Fondly,
Wendy and Tom

Dear Sean and Sue,

What an excellent, impromptu get-together that was last night! It's so fun when these last-minute plans really work out. The kids loved playing in the yard and going into town with Eric and Elliot, and we're always delighted to catch up with you and reconnect. We'll have to do it again soon. Thanks for being great hosts, great neighbors, and great friends.

Love,
Emily and Mark

Dear Patty and Michael,

Lionel and I wanted to thank you again for inviting us to your dinner party to meet Holly Guilford. It's inspiring to meet someone who not only wants to make a difference in our community but has the ideas and the support of local businesses to actually make them happen. We enjoyed everything about the evening, from the great food to the refreshing conversation. It was generous and kind of you to host such an elegant and entertaining event.

Thanks again.

Sincerely,
Lionel and Lisa Ross

Kindnesses

Unexpected kindnesses merit a thank-you note. Some examples are: if someone clips an article for you, fills in for you at work at the last minute, watches your kids one morning when you have an emergency doctor's appointment, waters your plants, or cares for your pet while you're away for the weekend.

Dear Darlene,

You are a doll. The plants are as perky as they were when I left on Friday. Thanks so much for taking the time over the weekend to visit my place and water everyone who needed to be watered. Please let me know when I can return the favor.

Yours,
Judy

Dear Melissa,

Thanks so much for looking after Spot last weekend while we were visiting Hal's parents in Virginia. I can't tell you how much it means to know that he's being cared for by a conscientious, intelligent, and caring young woman. Knowing that he's in such good hands means I don't have to worry every other minute over his well-being. Indeed, Spot seemed extremely content when we walked in the door on Sunday. Thanks again—we look forward to seeing you next weekend at your parents' party.

All the best,
Jardine

Dear Frances,

What a wonderful colleague and friend you are. Just knowing that the Henderson account was in your capable hands made my convalescence so much easier. Your help allowed me to concentrate on getting well, which I'm sure speeded up my recovery.

Thank you for covering my workload during my absence and know that I'm always ready to pitch in whenever you need a hand.

Best,
Joanna

Dear Eileen,

Now that John is home and recuperating, I finally have a quiet minute to write and tell you how indebted I am to you for looking after Josie when I had to run to the hospital on Friday. You were a much-needed calm presence during a scary emergency. You are a great neighbor and a great friend, and I hope to never have to return this particular favor— but I want you to know that I'm here when and if you need me.

My best,
Polly

Dear Samantha,

Thank you so much for the copies of the photos you made for me. The boys and I had so much fun with you and your kids that lovely summer day, and the photos are a wonderful way for us to always remember it. I am going to frame the three pictures of the kids in the rollercoaster cars together as a montage and hang it on my photo wall, where we will see it all the time. What happy times!

Thanks again for taking the time to come visit us, and we sure hope you'll come again soon.

Love,
Melissa, Scott, and Edward

Dear Joe,

Thank you so much for the electric foot warmer you sent for my birthday. Knowing how cold I sometimes get here at night, your gift was very thoughtful—especially coming from someone who lives in Phoenix!

Here's hoping all is well with you and thanks again.

Fondly,
Ruth

"EXCUSE THE LENGTH OF THIS LETTER. I HAD NO TIME TO WRITE A SHORT ONE." *–Blaise Pascal*

Hospitality or "Bread-and-Butter" Letters

Bread-and-butter letters are letter of thanks written after you've been someone's guest for the night, week-end, or longer. These letters should be written within three days of returning from the visit. (This suits the letter writer best, anyway, since the letter is easiest to write when the experience is fresh in your mind.)

Compliment something specific about the beauty of his or her home as well as the experience—maybe she has an impressively comprehensive antique teacup collection. Remember to mention her talent of making her guests feel comfortable.

Words and phrases for bread-and-butter letters:
a memorable evening/weekend . . .
such a beautiful home. . .
made us feel so at home . . .
a welcome retreat from the real world . . .
have always wanted to visit that part of the world. . . .
such thoughtful touches around the house and in
    our room . . .
warm and gracious hosts . . .

Dear Rox,

Staying at your cozy beach cottage is always such a treat. I look forward to it every summer. You have such an effortless way of whipping up those amazing gourmet meals—you are truly gifted. Most of all, I look forward to these summer visits as an opportunity for us to catch up and reconnect after a busy year.

Thanks so much for once again being a hostess extraordinaire.

Love,
Sabrina

Dear Leona,

Kyle and I have always wanted to visit Newport, so we were thrilled when we received your invitation. We were even more thrilled when we arrived at your and Phil's warm welcome and beautiful home. Thank you so much for a weekend that far surpassed our expectations and for all of the thoughtful touches that marked your hospitality—the deliciously tender lobsters on Friday night, your insider's tour of Newport architecture, going out on the boat Sunday, the flowers in the bathroom!

We had a wonderful time, and we look forward to seeing you again soon.

All the best,
Molly

Dear Charlotte,

What a surprise to get the mail today and find the photos you sent of our weekend in Maine! I am so happy to have them as a memento. The boys had so much fun that weekend with your boys, and the photos remind us all of that. We all looked at photos together when they arrived and were laughing all over again about them capsizing the canoes. I love the pictures of them splashing around in the lake. I'm going to frame those and hang them in the den or kitchen, so we can see them all the time.

Thanks so much for taking the time to get extra copies and to send them. I hope all is well with you. We look forward to seeing you all again soon.

All best,
Beverly

Dear Anne,

Thank you for letting me bunk in your guest room during my recent trip to New York. It was wonderful to catch up with you in the evenings over some delicious bottles of wine— what a necessary counterbalance to the meetings I was sitting through all day! If only I could bring you with me on every business trip! I hope that I can return the favor the next time you're in D.C.

Fondly,
Lucy

"WHEN IT COMES TO LIFE, THE CRITICAL THING IS WHETHER YOU TAKE THINGS FOR GRANTED OR TAKE THEM WITH GRATITUDE." –*G.K. Chesteron*

GIFTS AND OTHER GESTURES

Dear Mom and Dad,

Thanks so much for making the past week in the Vineyard another one that we will always treasure. Once again, your generosity and excellent hosting skills are much appreciated by myself, Larry, and the boys. The daily visits to the beach were lovely, as were Dad's guided tours of the best spots on the island for finding shells.

And the feasts were quite amazing—I swear the boys start talking about lobster as soon as we close the car door and start on our journey to the ferry. They—and we—look forward to these visits all year. Anyway, the time went by too quickly, and we look forward to seeing you soon. Thanks again.

Much love,
Kimberly

Illness-related and Condolence Gifts or Assistance

After a death of a loved one, gifts, flowers, donations, condolence cards, and any assistance—for example, meal deliveries—should be answered with thank-you notes. A reasonable amount of time for completing and sending the notes is six to eight weeks following the funeral.

If the deceased was a public figure, or if there are a great deal of notes to be sent, a family may opt to send out engraved or printed thank-you notes. (For example, this is what first lady Jacqueline Kennedy did on the occasion of her husband President Kennedy's death.) These cards should be white or cream, with or without a black border, and printed in black ink. It's appropriate to write a line or two at the bottom with your signature. The handwritten note at the bottom can be short: "Your letter was a great comfort," or "Hearing from you meant so much."

If you send pre-printed cards, you should still send entirely handwritten thank-you notes to those who've truly gone above and beyond—the neighbor who walked your dog every night for two weeks because you could not; the friend who made sure the children were where they needed to be; the person who donated enough to start a scholarship fund. These can wait until after some time has passed.

A PRE-PRINTED ACKNOWLEDGMENT:

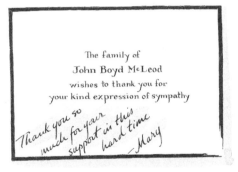

The family of
John Boyd McLeod
wishes to thank you for
your kind expression of sympathy

Thank you so much for your support in this hard time
— Mary

It's also acceptable for a widow to delegate the writing of thank-you notes to a family member or two following the death of his or her spouse. Some are too distraught to take on the task. For others, the writing of notes is a comfort. This personal note of thanks should follow the basic format—name the gift or kindness, make a personal connection between the gift and the person in whose memory it was given, and thank the recipient of the note for their thoughtfulness.

Words and phrases to express gratitude:
so thoughtful of you to think of us . . .
for your support and kindness throughout . . .
thank you for being there . . .
helping with all the details . . .
such a busy and sad few days. . . .
such a tough time for all of us . . .
we appreciated your kind words . . .
we appreciated your coming to sit with us. . . .

Dear Melissa,

Thank you so much for the wonderful home-cooked meal you brought over last week. I know I thanked you that evening, but I wanted to follow up with a note. It was so thoughtful of you to think of us and to intuit that the last thing we wanted to do that night was cook. Marvin always said that you are a wonderful friend, and of course he was right.

Warmly,
Janine

Dear Nina and Howard,

Thank you for the lovely arrangement you sent to our home last Saturday. Its lovely sight and smells continue to cheer me and the rest of the family during this sad time. I remember how Mom would scatter bunches of peonies around the house as soon as they were in-season. We all think of her and smile when we see the flowers you sent. It was so thoughtful of you to think of us.

Warmest wishes,
Hallie

Dear Melba and Lou,

Thank you so much for your donation to the American Cancer Society in Lizzie's name. The pain of losing her so young is often more than we can bear, but knowing that research is being funded that may one day prevent others from experiencing this kind of loss is comforting. Thank you for your generosity and support through everything.

Love,
Anne and Richard

Dear Father McNally,

Bob and I thank you for your support and consolation during this difficult time. The funeral service you performed gave inspiration and comfort to everyone present.

Sincerely,
Cathleen Pressman

CHAPTER FIVE

Thank-yous from Children and Teenagers

A s with piano or tennis, the earlier one begins to flex thank-you muscles, the easier and more automatic the gesture becomes. Of course, part of encouraging children to be grateful for what they receive is to lead by example. The other part is to let them know what's expected of them.

Before children learn to write, a parent should pen their notes for them. Thank-you notes written by a parent can be signed by either the parent or by both parent and child. It can be charming to have a toddler scribble something at the bottom of the note as long as it doesn't cover a great deal of the handwriting. Once the child is a little older and has practiced his signature, he can sign his name. Get your child in the practice of pondering why he's thankful for the gift by setting aside a time to sit down and "write" the notes together. Ask him to tell you why he likes each gift that he's received. Ask him to tell you what he'd like the gift giver to know. Use his words in the note, almost as if he is dictating to a secretary. Make the exercise fun, and the practice of appreciation will become automatic.

At about age six or seven, once a child has learned the basics of writing, she's ready to write her own thank-you notes. A parent can ease the way by writing a simple message that the child can copy: *Dear Nana, Thank you for the pretty Barbie. I really like her dress. Love, Abigail.* Once the child is a little older, she can be encouraged to be more creative, expressive, and specific in her thanks. Children have more freedom to be creative with their style of stationery and their use of language. In fact, a note that sounds too adult is not convincing.

THANK YOU NOTES FROM CHILDREN:

Dear Uncle Bob,

I've been playing the new Nintendo game you gave me nonstop since the party even though Mom keeps telling me to shut it off. I can't wait until you come over and we can play together. Thank you for the awesome birthday gift.

Love,
David

Dear Jeanette,

Thank you for coming to my party and for giving me the cool Bratz doll. I didn't have that one yet, and I really wanted it. It was fun having you at my party. I hope you had fun, too.

Your friend,
Denise

Dear Grandpa,

Thank you for the nice card and the birthday check. I don't know what I'm going to use it for yet, but I'll let you know when I decide. It'll be something good, I promise. I appreciate you remembering me every year on my birthday. You're a terrific grandfather, and I love you.

Love,
Liam

THANK-YOU NOTES FROM YOUNG CHILDREN:

Dear Aunt Marlene,

Thank you for the Power Ranger pajamas for my birthday. They are the best! Say hi to Sarah for me.

Love,
Shawn

Dear Danny,

Thank you for coming to my birthday party. You are my best friend. I can't wait to use the gift certificate for the toy store. I am going to buy the Star Wars video game. We can play it together.

Your friend,
Lee

THANK-YOUS FROM CHILDREN AND TEENAGERS

Dear Coach Gary,

I really liked softball this year. It was fun. You are a nice coach. I hope you are my coach next year.

Your friend,
Laura

THANK YOU NOTES FOR KINDNESSES SHOWN

Dear Dr. Jordan,

Thank you for being so nice to me when I broke my arm. I was scared, and you made me feel okay. You were right. It didn't hurt that much. I liked being able to pick out the color of my cast. You are a great doctor.

Thank you,
Rachel

THANK-YOUS FROM CHILDREN AND TEENAGERS

Dear Mrs. Quinn,

Thank you for being such a nice teacher. It was fun to be in your class. I am a little scared of going into third grade and seeing who my new teacher will be. Can I come visit you?

Thank you for the book about the dinosaurs. I like T-Rex the best. Do you?

Your student,
Chris Cooper

Dear Samantha,

I have so much fun when you babysit. You are the best! Thank you for bringing over your favorite movies to share with me and for teaching me the card trick.

Your friend,
Karen

THANK-YOUS FROM CHILDREN AND TEENAGERS

Thank-you Notes from Teenagers

Some of the first thank-you notes a child learns to write are for birthday gifts. Once kids become teenagers, they might start staying over at friends' houses or going away with friends' families on vacation. The "bread-and-butter" notes written following such visits are the next thank-you note milestone on the road to adulthood.

"THERE IS NOT A MORE PLEASING EXERCISE OF THE MIND THAN GRATITUDE. IT IS ACCOMPANIED WITH SUCH AN INWARD SATISFACTION THAT THE DUTY IS SUFFICIENTLY REWARDED BY THE PERFORMANCE."

–Joseph Addison

BREAD-AND-BUTTER LETTERS
FROM TEENAGERS:

Dear Mr. and Mrs. Kerner,

Thank you very much for inviting me to spend the week with you and Peter at your beautiful house in Aspen. As you know I love to ski, and it was such a treat to take those phenomenal runs each day with Peter. I couldn't believe the powder! Now that I'm home, I'm dreaming about it. I also enjoyed getting to know you better. Now I can see why Peter is so great.

Thanks again for your hospitality.

Sincerely,
Matt

Dear Dr. Bailey and Mr. Wilson,

As always, I had a terrific time staying at your house. You have the best movie collection in town, and your ice cream selection isn't bad, either. You're very generous to let me hang out over there so much with Jamie and Jason, and I appreciate it.

Sincerely,
Carter

———

Dear Grandma and Grandpa,

Thank you for taking care of me while my mom and dad were away. I love staying at your house. You make the best pancakes, and as always, your meals were feasts. The time went by so quickly; I'm already looking forward to seeing you at Thanksgiving.

Thanks again for everything,
Calvin

A Note on Teens

During adolescence, children make the transition from colorful, whimsical stationery to more mature styles of letter paper and note cards. Teenagers have less leeway as far as how late they can slide before sending their thank-yous. Teens should be encouraged to act as adults and to write thank-you notes promptly and more articulately than they did during their younger years. A teen can't get away with writing every note with the beginning, "Thank you for the [blank]." Encourage them to put more effort into their letters.

"PLEASE WRITE AGAIN SOON. THOUGH MY OWN
LIFE IS FILLED WITH ACTIVITY, LETTERS ENCOURAGE
MOMENTARY ESCAPE INTO OTHERS LIVES AND I COME
BACK TO MY OWN WITH GREATER CONTENTMENT."

–Elizabeth Forsythe Hailey

CHAPTER SIX

Business Correspondence

HANDWRITTEN NOTE STANDS out in the business world because it's in contrast to a sea of typed, formal correspondence, both on paper and onscreen. As in the social realm, a handwritten note indicates you have put more thought and care into its crafting beyond the generic communiqués that punctuate daily office life. Making this effort is recommended when a person has gone out of his or her way to benefit you and your business. This might include a job interview, referral, mentorship, recommendation, major purchase by a customer, hosting you at a business-related social event, or business gifts and entertainment. Other situations that merit a thank-you note include volunteer work toward an organization or the gift of a charitable contribution.

Business-related Thank-you Basics
The basic format for business thank-yous stays true to the general thank-you note format.

Salutation.
Mention the gift or kindness.
Personalize the note by writing how you feel about it. (Why was the job interview so informative? Why was the Christmas gift so well-suited to you and your wife?)
Say "thank you."
The wind-up.
Closing.

Writing business correspondence can be intimidating because you have more at stake. You don't want your tone to be misconstrued. You need to walk the line between grateful and sycophantic, confident and cocky, firm and overbearing. Especially when the person to whom you're writing has control over your fate, take extra care with your word choice, spelling, and grammar. You should still be yourself and let your personality come through. It's fine to sound conversational and friendly.

Special concerns regarding business correspondence
- Make sure you have the person's title and name correct. Check their business card and, if you have any correspondence from them, check to see how they address themselves.
- Write neatly. Make sure your writing is legible.
- Don't write anything that you would be embarrassed to have read aloud.
- Think carefully before you promise anything.
- Avoid using slang or jargon.
- It's fine to use a little humor, especially if you are rehashing something you laughed about together and/or if you know the recipient has a good sense of humor. But proceed with extreme caution and make

no remark that could be misinterpreted and only if you are writing about matters that are not grave.

- Proofread these notes a few more times than you would a regular thank-you note. Consider letting someone you trust proofread it as well.
- Make a copy of the note before you send it out.

Words and phrases for business-related gratitude:
for taking the time to talk with me about . . .
your excellent overview of the company . . .
of the responsibilities associated with the position . . .
for making this opportunity possible . . .
for helping me transition my career . . .
for the wonderful things you have taught me . . .
for your perspective and advice . . .

A Note about Salutation

If you're not sure how to address the recipient, err on the side of formality, i.e., "Dear Mr. Jones" or "Dear Ms. Jones." If they are more of a peer than a superior, but you have not yet been introduced, you can use the full name, i.e., "Dear Matthew Jones" or "Dear Michelle Jones."

Interview Thank-yous

Notes thanking your interviewer should be written the same day as the interview and sent that day or first thing the next morning. You should mention something specific you discussed during the interview to show that you paid attention. This will also help the interviewer remember you. If you're interested in the job, you can tie it to one of your strengths to stress you're particularly suited to the position.

E-mailed Thank-you Notes

A handwritten thank-you note signals to the receiver that you are a savvy, competent, and intelligent individual. When in doubt, default to the written thank-you note. However, individual savvy is also important, and there are certain situations that call for quicker action. For example, you might be attending a business or law school where recruiters visit a few times a year to conduct tens of interviews per day—and decide that night who they will choose to invite back for the second round. Sending a handwritten thank-you note to the recruiter's out-of-town office will result in him or her receiving the note long after the decisions about the next round have been made.

This is why it's vital to ask about the interview process: "When will you be holding second round interviews?" "How quickly will you be making a decision?" If there's a tight timeframe, take the "belt and braces" approach. Belt and braces is when the candidate sends an e-mail thank-you note immediately to thank the interviewer for his/her time and mentions in the e-mail that an official thank-you note has been written and sent to their office.

If you do opt to write a thank-you e-mail, remember that although the medium feels informal, you should never stray from a strictly professional tone.

A surefire "don't" is to only send an e-mail—this sends the entirely unimpressive message that you care enough to do the very least.

A BELTS AND BRACES THANK-YOU:

Dear Mr. Candless,

Thank you for your time today. I enjoyed learning more about Cooper, Wick & Gump, specifically about how the extent of your work this past year has involved procuring patents for technological firms. Our talk confirmed for me that my background in computer science—and my desire to continue working with technology—makes me a good fit for Cooper, Wick & Gump. I was especially interested to find out that I've worked in the past with a few of your clients, including Gomad and JWT.

I've also sent a letter to your office, but I wanted to send this quick note of appreciation today. I look forward to hearing from you.

Sincerely,
Harold Jones

SAMPLE THANK-YOU LETTERS:

Dear Ms. Hyde,

I learned a great deal today while talking with you about the editorial assistant position at Big House Press. I was interested to hear that your assistants are asked to weigh in on selections from the slush pile. As we talked about, my ultimate goal is to become an acquisitions editor, and I understand that reading and assessing unsolicited manuscripts is great training for such a career. Thank you so much for taking the time to talk with me. I look forward to hearing from you soon.

Sincerely,
Jonathan Michelson

Dear Steve,

Thank you for taking the time to meet with me today. I enjoyed learning more about the school's pedagogy, and watching some classes in progress was an unexpected treat. Pritzker Prep's emphasis on creative thinking and on nurturing independent minds aligns completely with my own philosophy and with my experience at Indian Mountain Day School. I look forward to hearing what you and the English department decide.

Sincerely,
Eloise

Dear Jill,

Thank you for taking the time to have lunch with me on Tuesday. It was very helpful for me to learn what you think are the real strengths and weaknesses of our industry, and how we should position our company with these factors in mind. I came back from lunch recharged to make some improvements with a new perspective on things.

I truly appreciate your advice and assistance.

Sincerely,
Connie

THANK-YOU NOTE FOR A REFERRAL:

Dear Genevieve,

Thank you for passing my name along to John Smalls at Marsh, Klipton and Young. I appreciate your generosity of spirit, and I'm flattered that you think enough of my work to recommend me to a colleague. I look forward to seeing you at Wednesday's meeting.

Gratefully,
George

T&C Tip: *Even if you don't want the job, you should write a thank-you note to the interviewer. You never know when you might meet that person again at some future point in your career.*

THANK-YOU NOTE FOR A MENTORSHIP:

Dear Ms. Hyde,

I think I could have continued to fire questions at you for another two hours this afternoon. It was so helpful for me to hear your take on Glaxo's strengths and weaknesses and on its role in the current climate. Thank you so much for taking time out of your busy schedule to talk with me. I came back to the office recharged and newly focused on making some improvements. I've already brainstormed a few different strategies for rehauling the accounting system.

Thank you again—I truly appreciate your advice and counsel.

Respectfully,
Andrew

THANK-YOU NOTE FOR LUNCH:

Dear Cassandra,

Thank you for lunch yesterday. I was delighted to meet you and to hear about your exciting project. It sounds like your venture is off to a great start. I look forward to talking with you in a few months to revisit how Gidget PR might help you bring your message to your desired demographic. Have a wonderful time in South Africa.

All the best,
Kiki

THANK-YOU TO A COMMITTEE LEADER FOR HER HARD WORK:

Dear Miranda,

Your hard work and creative talents made last Wednesday's fundraiser a great success. Numerous people have approached me to let me know that this year's event was second to none. I don't have to tell you that you and your committee accomplished nothing short of a miracle—but I will, anyway! So many thanks for your dedication, professionalism, and commitment. I hope that we have an opportunity to work together again in the near future.

Yours,
Harvey

THANK-YOU NOTE FOR A GIFT:

Dear Phyllis,

My wife and I have always loved attending the opera, but the tickets you gave us made the experience even more enjoyable than usual. From where we were sitting we could see the anguish and the joy in each actor's expressions. I think we could even see the perspiration on the tenor's brow when he hit the High C. What a truly exceptional evening. Thanks so much for thinking of us.

Sincerely,
James

Improving Your Handwriting

NO MATTER YOUR AGE, it's possible to improve your handwriting. As you replicate the sentence on the following pages, remember to use your shoulder and forearm muscles to write, holding your fingers and wrist stiff.

The quick brown fox jumps over the lazy dog.

The quick brown fox
jumps over the lazy dog.

RESOURCES

Below is a short list of titles on the topics of letter writing and etiquette. Hundreds of books on both of these topics can be found in libraries, bookstores, and through Internet retailers.

Brosseau, Jim, ed. *Town & Country Social Graces: Words of Wisdom on Civility in a Changing Society.* NY: Sterling Publishing Co., Inc., 2002.

Editors of *Victoria* Magazine. *Writing Personal Notes and Letters.* NY: Sterling Publishing Co., Inc., 1998.

Farley, Thomas P., ed. *Town & Country Modern Manners: The Thinking Person's Guide to Social Graces.* NY: Sterling Publishing Co., Inc., 2005.

Martin, Judith. *Miss Manners' Guide to Excruciatingly Correct Behavior.* NY: Warner Books, 1982.

Martin, Judith. *Miss Manners' Guide for the Turn-of-the-Millennium.* NY: Pharos Books, 1989.

Post, Elizabeth L. *Emily Post on Etiquette.* NY: Harper & Row, 1987.

Post, Emily. *Etiquette in Society, in Business, in Politics, and at Home.* NY: Funk & Wagnalls, 1922.

INDEX

INDEX